Siberian Husky Problems: The A to Z of Siberian Husky Behavior

Mark Mathis

Mark Mathis

ISBN: 1530919436
ISBN-13: 978-1530919437

DISCLAIMER AND LEGAL NOTICE:

CONTENTS

	Why I Wrote This Book	i
1	Crafting The Perfect Husky	1
2	A is for Aggression	2
3	C is for Charging at the Door	8
4	D is for Digging	9
5	E is for Escaping or Running Away	10
6	F is for Fear and Fighting	11
7	H is for Hunting Smaller Animals	14
8	J is for Jumping on People	15
9	S is for Separation Anxiety and Submission	16
10	What is Your Husky Trying to Tell You?	20
10	Conclusion	23

WHY I WROTE THIS BOOK

First of all let me say thank you for reading this book. I hope it provides all the information you are looking for to take care of your new family member. I wrote this book out of my love for Siberian Huskies and the need for a beginner's guide to owning one. This is not one of those fill in the blank dog breed books that you see for sale online. This is truly a Siberian Husky only book and will always be. I will update this title from time to time as well as create more books in the future on other aspects of owning a Siberian Husky.

We want this book to be a resource for problems while training their new Siberian Husky puppy by covering:

- Digging
- Jumping Up
- Charging the Door
- Running Away
- Hunting Smaller Animals
- Separation Anxiety
- Fighting Other Dogs

This book is for all of the Siberian Husky lovers out there.

You can find more information and tips on raising your Husky at:

www.siberianhuskypuppytraining.com/newsletter

Thank You

CRAFTING THE PERFECT HUSKY

So, you've welcomed a husky into your life – and what a great choice you've made. Huskies can be the most friendly and loving asset to your family. However, sometimes this great asset needs a little work to enable them to fit into your home.

If you've bought a husky puppy or rescue dog and you're now faced with behavioral issues that you need to address, you're in luck. The A-Z of Husky Behavior is here to help!

With the help of this manual, you'll be able to identify your problems and implement the right solutions, making your husky a valued, loving member of your household. For ease of reading, this book will refer to your husky as 'he'. These tips, however, are applicable to both sexes of husky.

A IS FOR … AGGRESSION

While they can make the friendliest of pets, huskies may be more inclined towards dominance than other breeds of dog. This breed is reared to work in packs, each one with its own alpha leader. Whether they're being use as working dogs or living in the wild, most huskies will be instinctively inclined to following a hierarchical structure.

While not all huskies will experience dominance problems, if your husky does, he will certainly not be alone. If you have had your husky from a puppy, you may have shown him enough positive socialization to avoid dominance issues. However, if you have opened your heart and home to a rescue dog who has been neglected or abused in the past, or you were not fully knowledgeable on your puppy's needs when you got him, your husky may need help and rehabilitation to enable him to socialize well with others, and become a safe, integrated member of your loving home.

The first and most important step is to recognize the dominant behavior. Seeing and understanding the behavior is foundation of managing it. Let's look at some different forms of dominance that your husky may display. We'll look at each one individually so that you can identify the signs.

AGGRESSIVE DOMINANCE

Aggressive dominance is your husky's way of exercising control over the humans or animals in his presence. Your dog may be feeling threatened and may ready himself to attack. In this situation, do not allow yourself or others to be within the biting range of your dog. He poses a potentially dangerous threat to you, your loved ones or other animals. Please use caution when dealing with an aggressive husky, as there is always a cause and solution for his behavior.

SIGNS TO LOOK OUT FOR

The signs of aggression may manifest themselves early in your dog's life. Your dog may display aggression by growling, snapping and even biting. With puppies, this may be noticeable when you approach their food bowl or try to take a toy from them. These early signs of aggressive dominance should not be ignored in your puppy, or they will get worse as the dog grows up.

In your adult husky, you will notice aggression in the following ways:

- Your husky will stand erect and stiff, making himself appear as large as he can, raising his head and stretching upwards as though on his toes.
- While in this rigid stance he is likely to be leaning forward as though he is poised to prance on the subject he is to dominate.
- His weight will be on the front legs, his hair (hackles) will be raised on his back and near his tail.
- His ears will be pointing forward and he will be looking directly at his target.
- You will see his stiff tail raised high in the air and it may shake from side to side slightly.
- He will be growling or barking aggressively while showing his teeth with his lips curled.
- His nose and forehead may show wrinkles as well.
- This stance is not unlike the stance that a human might take if they are threatened. It is an attempt to appear as menacing as possible.

THE SOLUTION

Ultimately, with huskies (as with any other dog) you need to be the alpha in your home. All dogs accept the hierarchy that is natural to pack dogs; there is a leader who is to be pleased, and subordinates that are to be dominated. While it may seem cruel to enforce dominance over your dog, this is an accepted and expected group dynamic that your husky will recognize, and that will result in a happier home for you and your husky.

Aggressive behavior must be checked as soon as it arises.

Depending on the degree of aggression your husky displays, there are things you may be able to do yourself. However, if these do not work, be prepared to consult a behavior specialist or an obedience school. If you're going to have the happy life you want for you husky and family, then deal with this behavior as soon as you notice it.

Your first action is for you to adopt the strong alpha role that places you as the leader in your household:

- Avoid game playing with your husky which allows him to win.
- Feeding time for your dog should come noticeably after your own. You are the alpha dog and you eat first.
- Go through doors ahead of your husky, showing you're superior place in the household hierarchy.
- If your dog is in the way, make him move, do not go around him.
- Call your dog to you for petting, don't go to him.
- Wait for your dog to greet you when you come home, do not go looking for him.
- Do not let your dog decide which rules he complies with. All rules laid out by you are law.
- Do not allow your husky to sleep in your bed as this implies his equality to you. Once you've established yourself as the leader, you can relax this rule if you wish to.
- Never reward aggressive behavior, always reward compliance.

If necessary, purchase a muzzle to use in instances where your dog usually shows signs of aggression. Neutering a male husky will lower his testosterone and often helps with aggression.

In addition to this, increasing your husky's exercise routine will result in a tired dog, with fewer energy reserves, making him less likely to want to take an aggressive stance.

PASSIVE DOMINANCE

When your husky displays passive dominance, he is usually trying to establish dominance over another dog without initiating an attack. However, if neither dog backs down from this stance, one dog may then switch to being aggressive which may lead to a fight. Keep a watchful eye on your husky to make sure he plays safe with others.

SIGNS TO LOOK OUT FOR
The signs of this type of dominance are to be seen in your husky's posture:

- He will be stiff legged while staring at his target.
- He may try to stretch in order to be taller than his target.

- His ears will be forward and his mouth will be closed unless he is panting.
- He may not wrinkle his muzzle while he investigates his target, but you may hear a slight growl.

THE SOLUTION
If the aggression is simply barking, then you can choose to ignore it – it may simply be a demand for attention. When he stops, give lots of praise so he recognizes that this is the behavior that pleases you.

TERRITORIAL AGGRESSION

Territorial aggression is born out of the dog's belief that the home and yard is his possession, much like his food bowl and toys. Anybody coming on to his territory is a potential threat. Some dogs will work out for themselves that the mailman is not a threat. Others will look to your reaction for guidance. If you are fearful, they will read this and perceive the visitor as a foe rather than a friend.

SIGNS TO LOOK OUT FOR
The behavior of the territorial dog will be much the same as the dominant aggressive husky. He will react in much the same way, taking a similar stance.

THE SOLUTION
Once you establish the alpha role, your husky will look to you for instruction when a stranger is present.

Socializing your dog early will establish confidence in your husky. If it is safe to do so, encourage friends and family to take your husky on short walks so that he recognizes that most people are safe and not to be seen as a threat.

It is essential to establish early on that your dog is not the owner of your home – you are. Anything that your dog has is gifted to him by you. If your husky understands that he has no possessions, he will have no need for territorial action.

PREDATORY AGGRESSION

As a working dog breed, huskies tend to have strong prey urges. This is a natural instinct and needs to be recognized and addressed whenever you notice it.

SIGNS TO LOOK OUT FOR
Your husky, upon seeing small children and animals moving at speed/playing, may charge and launch himself into the middle of these situations.

THE SOLUTION
Your husky must be shown firmly that this is not acceptable behavior. Direct supervision of your dog within environments where this is likely to happen is a must. All family members must practice obedience training.

Your dog must know that in the hierarchy of the household, he is at the bottom. Usually a sharp command of "NO" is sufficient to stop this behavior.

OFFENSIVE AGGRESSION

Offensive aggression is a manifestation of confidence and anger, in addition to aggressive feelings. The overconfidence makes your dog likely to attack if not stopped in his tracks. Any attack is likely to be intense as he believes he will win. This kind of aggression puts both animals and humans at risk of being bitten.

SIGNS TO LOOK OUT FOR
- Your husky will fix his gaze upon his targeted human or animal.
- His head will be held up high with ears erect and pointing forward. His tail will be raised and rigid and may wag stiffly.
- Hair (hackles) will be raised along the length of his back.
- Your dog will use threatening tones, growling, barking and snarling at his target.
- Like many of the aggressive stances discussed, your dog will look ready to pounce with weight on front legs. If an attack takes place, it will be determined and relentless.

THE SOLUTION
As with all aggressive behavior, you need to establish a strong leadership role that ensures that in these situations you are in charge and able to give a command to cease.

DEFENSIVE AGGRESSION

If your husky is scared, he may go into a defensive stance.
He is likely to feel uncertain about his actions. He would prefer not to take

action, but a continued feeling of being threatened may cause him to do so. Biting may take place so use caution.

SIGNS TO LOOK OUT FOR

- In this stance, he will keep his body low to the ground with his head also held low.
- He may have his hackles raised, but he may not.
- He will be looking at the source of fear with wide eyes and dilated pupils.
- He will lay his ears back flat against his head.
- He could possibly be showing his teeth, slightly curling his lips and having some wrinkles in the muzzle area.
- His tail will be motionless, tucked between his legs
- Your husky may stand tall with his weight evenly distributed across all four legs.
- He will attempt to look tall, with his head held erect and stiff. His tail will be rigid and erect and his hackles will stand up.
- His vocal warnings of barks, snarls and growls will be slightly higher in pitch than his offensive aggressive bark.

Your husky will be feeling a combination of emotions. Anger, fear and aggression will result in body language that is associated with fear and offensive aggression.

The closer in proximity to the target your dog is, the more likelihood of an attack. The likelihood of an attack taking place also hinges on the perceived threat, and his confidence at that time, making his behavior unpredictable.

THE SOLUTION

Defensive aggression is most common in huskies who are not well socialized and have a poor ability to read situations. Your husky needs to be imbued with the skills to read and deal with the stress of new situations. Obedience training will give your dog more confidence so that he does not feel the need to defend himself against every new person or animal he meets.

C IS FOR … CHARGING AT THE DOOR

You may find that every time you open your door, your husky bolts for it in an attempt to get outside.

THE SOLUTION

You need to teach your husky that good behavior means he'll get to go outside to run and play, and misbehavior means he will not get to go out at all.

Start by calling your dog to you by name. Give him the "Sit" command, and reward him with a treat for waiting. If he's too excited to wait, simply ignore him and walk away, trying again after a while. If he stays put, put on his collar and leash. If he tries to jump on you, or play while trying to put on the collar, give him a firm "NO" command followed by another "Sit" command. After he has his collar and leash on you can open the door. If he stands up before you are ready to leave, give him a "NO" command and close the door. Wait until he's calm and sitting again before opening the door. If he remains seated while the door is open you can give him permission to come with you.

As with all training, this may take some practice. Thankfully, once your husky knows that he will be rewarded for good behavior with outdoor time, he will remember.

D IS FOR … DIGGING

Huskies love to dig. In their natural habitat, you'll find them digging holes into the snow to keep warm. Sometimes they dig because they've smelled something in the ground that they are trying to get to. Never yell at or hit your husky for digging. You can easily redirect his energy elsewhere. Remember: you are the alpha, and you have to be smarter than your husky.

THE SOLUTION
Make a sandbox or a designated area in the yard for digging. If you catch your Husky digging elsewhere give him a firm "NO" and lead him over to the designated area. You can bury treats in this designated area to help assist and reward your husky for digging in the right area.

If he continues to dig elsewhere you can bury some of his feces in his holes. When he digs the holes back up, he will not like the surprise.

If all else fails, another option is to put socks on your husky's front feet to prevent him from digging while he's outside. While it is not the best long term option, it has worked for other owners.

E IS FOR ... ESCAPING OR RUNNING AWAY

Siberian huskies were bred to run, and the only way to ensure their safety is to keep them on a leash and have a secure backyard.

THE SOLUTION

Make sure that your fence is at least 6 feet high, though preferably higher. Huskies are known to dig underneath a fence as well jumping over it, so you will need to implement a deterrence for this as well.

One way is to bury a concrete wall, or use cinder blocks underneath the fence to prevent them from digging out. Chicken wire can also be used.

Working sled dogs are often tethered when not racing. You may wish to try this for your husky, but you must be certain that your backyard is safe before doing so. A tethered dog may not be able to escape from a threat.

F IS FOR … FEAR

Fearful dogs are terrified of being attacked and harmed. A rescue dog that has suffered abuse from a previous owner may be more likely to behave in a fearful manner.

SIGNS TO LOOK OUT FOR

If your husky is being fearful, he will exhibit many of the same behaviors as in a fearful dominant state, but there are likely to be some additional signs such as:

- He may be panting heavily with a wrinkled or tight mouth. He may also whine or yap.
- In order to display to his target a lack of threat, he may take a shrinking stance.
- He will lower his body to the ground, appearing smaller in order to convey an unthreatening position.
- He may roll over showing submission and avoid eye contact, which he fears will be seen as confrontational.
- His eyes may move to the side, showing whiter areas, and he may blink more.
- His muscles will be tense and if very scared he may empty his bowels and urinate.
- He may be trembling with a hunched back with low tail tucked down, and his head may hang low with flattened ears.
- His body may lean to one side as though ready to recoil from any attack.

Your Husky will be more likely to flee or hide from the source of his fear, rather than bite and attack. However, if backed into a corner or given no escape, he could escalate his behavior to a more aggressive state. He may snap or attempt to deliver a brisk bite before trying to escape.

THE SOLUTION

Many fearful huskies are born with a tendency towards shyness. However, as previously mentioned, a rescue dog may have other reasons for his fear.

Build confidence in your dog with praise and reassurance, rewarding him with treats and petting when he is obedient. If your dog is not too shy, an obedience school will be helpful in dealing with fear.

When your dog approaches you, try not to make sudden movements and avoid making loud noises that are likely to alarm him. He is unlikely to bite unless he is scared and feels threatened.

Desensitizing your dog to the things that normally scare him will help him to realize that these situations are not to be feared. You will be aiming to turn these fear-inducing situations into positive ones. Love and patience along with consistency and obedience training should help your husky to overcome his anxiety and have a happy life.

F IS FOR ... FIGHTING

If your husky gets into a serious fight with another dog it's important to have a plan of action. Never grab a dog's collar or neck during a fight. They may turn to attack you instead, thinking you are another threat trying to harm them.

THE SOLUTION

Grab his back legs right where they connect to the body. Once you've got a hold, you will lift him in a wheelbarrow fashion and firmly drag them backwards away from the other dog. With the front legs being the dog's only support, it is less likely to turn and risk falling.

If you are not alone, get somebody to do the same to the other dog.

After you've dragged the dogs apart, you will need to turn their bodies around 180 degrees so that they cannot see each other, enabling them to calm down.

Hopefully, the dog your husky was fighting with will have an owner who will assist in breaking the fight up. If you're alone, it is important to use extreme caution when trying to separate them. Breaking up a fight alone is dangerous and puts you at risk of being bitten.

In a worst-case scenario in which your dog fights while you are alone, grab a leash and run it around the back loin, threading the leash back through the handle. Use the leash to drag the dog, like you would with your hands, to a location that you can tie it to. Once you have leased one dog, grab the other dog by the back legs, as instructed, and drag it away, turning it around so that the dogs can't see each other and are able to calm down.

Anyone who walks your dog should be made aware of these instructions for their own safety.

H IS FOR ... HUNTING SMALLER ANIMALS

Siberian huskies have a high prey drive and will generally try to kill anything smaller than them that passes their line of sight.

THE SOLUTION
It is paramount to socialize your husky at a young age, with all the animals that it will normally see during its lifetime.

If you adopt an older Siberian husky, take care to keep them on a leash and away from other people's pets, as this hunting behavior is extremely hard to remove from older dogs.

J IS FOR ... JUMPING ON PEOPLE

Huskies, like many dogs, are sometimes overzealous and over familiar. This leads them to jump up at people. Jumping that relates to dominance should be dealt with using the solution in the aggressive dominance section. Other types of jumping can be solved as follows.

THE SOLUTION

The solution here is to reward the good behavior and ignore the bad. This works best if your husky knows the command "Sit", but you can still use it if he doesn't.

If you find that your husky likes to jump on you as you come in the door, or in any other situation, this has a simple fix. Be sure to have some treats with you for this. When your husky tries to jump up, simply side step so they can't jump on you. Ignore them completely, even if they continue jumping. Avoiding eye contact is especially important. Siberian Huskies are social animals and they will take being ignored as a negative stimulus.

Once you husky has calmed down, say "Down" while lowering a treat to the floor. After he follows the treat with his nose, place it on the floor and give him your affection. You'll want to issue the "Sit" command after, and reward him with your verbal praise.

You should practice this every day until your husky knows that staying down will produce a desirable outcome for him, which is your love and attention.

S IS FOR … SEPARATION ANXIETY

Your husky has an innate nature as a pack animal, and he will long to have company at all times. If he were in a pack in the wild, he would never be left alone. You may find that your husky becomes anxious when you (acting as your husky's "pack") have to leave him alone. This can lead to howling, barking, leaping, chewing on objects or even escaping.

As unfortunate as it may be, you will need to leave your dog at times, and you want it to be as stress-free as possible for both you and your husky. If you recognize any of these symptoms of separation anxiety, immediately begin working with some of the solutions listed.

SIGNS TO LOOK OUT FOR
Signs of separation anxiety are usually evident early and are as follows:

- When you start to leave your husky begins to howl or whine and tries to keep your attention.
- Your husky begins to act badly when you are trying to leave. He may be doing so for attention.
- Your husky begins trembling and whining when he thinks you are about to leave him.
- Your husky stays extremely close to you every moment while you are home out of fear that you might leave him.
- Your husky is already house trained but starts to relieve himself in the house constantly.

THE SOLUTION

Start desensitizing your dog to you leaving. For example, go through your regular ritual before leaving, but simply sit down instead. Repeat this a few times so that your husky will get comfortable with you leaving the house.

After he's calm about you getting your things, start walking outside as well, and come back into the house after a minute or two. Repeat this until he's relaxed with the idea of you going outside.

After he's calm with you leaving for about twenty minutes, you can start circling the block in your car, or by foot, and then coming back. Doing these exercises will gradually let your dog know that you will always come back. It will also help him to get used to being left alone.

When you return home, do not pay attention to your dog until he's calm and laying or sitting down. This will help him remain calm about you leaving, rather than getting into an excited state.

You may wish to exercise your dog before you leave. This will give him time to go to the bathroom and release any pent up energy that may be lurking inside. Be sure to exercise him when you get home as well.

If your husky sleeps in a crate while you're away, be sure to put an interactive play toy inside with him along with an article of clothing that has your scent to keep him company.

On example of a good toy is a Kong stuffed with food or treats to keep him busy for a while.

S IS FOR … SUBMISSIVE BEHAVIORS

Submissive behavior is your husky's way of telling you, the alpha, that he recognizes you as a leader. You want your dog to show you submission. The hope is that he will not behave this way towards an aggressive dog that is about to attack him.

We will look at the types of submission your husky may show and the signs to look for in this section.

PASSIVE SUBMISSION

SIGNS TO LOOK OUT FOR
- In this stance, your husky will have his body lowered with his head turned away from the target.
- His ears will be slightly back and his mouth closed unless he's panting.
- He will keep his muzzle smooth to allow the other dog to smell him first.
- His tail will be relaxed in its normal position.

ACTIVE SUBMISSION

SIGNS TO LOOK OUT FOR
- This position is similar to passive submission, but he may begin to lick his target's chin, whether it be another dog or you.
- He may give brief eye contact and keep his tail low to the ground.
- You may also hear your husky whine a little.

TOTAL SUBMISSION

SIGNS TO LOOK OUT FOR

In this position, your husky will give over complete control.

- He will be lying on his back with his stomach and throat exposed.
- His head will be turned, avoiding eye contact.
- He may urinate a little.
- While in this position he may allow other dogs or humans to stand over him allowing them to show dominance.
- He may whine or yelp a little while holding his tail between his legs as far as it will go.

WHAT IS YOUR SIBERIAN HUSKY PUPPY TRYING TO TELL YOU?

Since your Siberian Husky puppy can't speak to you it's important to know their body language. You can learn a lot about what your Husky is feeling or thinking simply by observing how they move.

BOWING

If you catch your Husky bowing down at you with their tail wagging then they are telling you they are ready to play. So grab a toy and go have fun!

NUDGING YOU

If your Husky nudges or hits you with their nose, they are trying to get you to play with them. Where bowing would be asking for you to play nudging is their way of demanding your attention. Huskies that are more dominant than others are likely to do this.

HOLDING YOUR HAND

To show their affection for you, your Husky may try to hold your hand in their mouth. This is an important bonding activity that you should take part in as it's their way of telling you to trust them and that they will not bite you.

LICKING OR BITING

Be sure to keep an eye out for this. If they are simply licking or biting the base of their tail they could have fleas. If they continue doing so for prolonged periods of time however, it could be a compulsive behavior. Be sure and speak to your veterinarian on treatment so your Husky will not begin to get raw or bleed from those areas.

HEAD TILTING

This is a universal sign for a curious or puzzled dog. With Huskies being naturally curious animals, you may see this a lot, unless they are sick and are showing other symptoms.

SNIFFING or CIRCLING

This is how all dogs greet each other they may start at one end and work their way to the other. You may catch them sniffing humans as well.

MOUNTING

If your Husky is trying to mount another dog or a human, it is usually more of a dominant behavior. That is their way of showing their power over others. If you have done your job of becoming the pack leader you shouldn't have to worry about this.

PAWING

Your Husky may try to place their paw over the shoulder of other dogs in an effort to establish dominance over them. They will also do this by placing their chin over other dogs.

TAIL

You can learn a lot from your Husky simply by observing their tail. They will usually leave their tail down and keep it relaxed. If you see them curl up their tail then they are excited, when they wag their tail it's the same as if they are smiling or could also be nervousness depending on the situation. If their tail is erect and has a shorter arc it may be a sign of dominant aggression. If they hold their tail between their legs than they are being submissive or fearful.

SLEEPING STYLE

Paying attention to how your Husky sleeps can also give you a clue to how they are feeling. For instance if your Husky is cold they may curl up and use their tail to cover their nose keeping it warm. This is commonly called the Siberian Swirl.

If you see your Husky yawning they may not exactly be tired. Yawns can also indicate tension or anxiety. You can watch your Husky before a walk or ride in the car to see if they are feeling anxious about anything and help them feel relaxed.

If you find your Husky snuggled up close to you, they're probably not trying to keep warm as their bodies are warmer than yours.

Most likely they're trying to feel safe in your presence. If they are more of an alpha dog they may keep a little more distant from you signifying that they like feeling secure but can protect themselves. Of course the less dominant your Husky is the closer they may sleep near you.

You may find your Husky lying flat on their stomach with their legs spread out. Don't worry they're just hot and trying to dissipate their body heat. If you find your Husky sleeping on their back with their legs in the air, then you can rest easy as well because you have a happy, care free and self-assured dog. Your Husky puppy experiences (REM) or rapid eye movement just like humans do. Do not disturb your Husky while they are dreaming as they could be experiencing a nightmare. Even the calmest dog can snap at you if you wake them at the wrong time.

RECOGNIZING PAIN

Your Husky will try hard to hide their pain, but it's your job as their owner to recognize signs of pain in order to help them feel better. Even the slightest difference in their walk could signify something is wrong so be sure and pay attention to your Siberian Husky puppy.

You can use this list of symptoms to determine if you need to take your Husky to your vet immediately for help.

- A loss of appetite
- Favoring a specific part of the body
- The sight of blood on your Husky or the floor
- Any kind of swelling
- Acting more aggressive or more timid
- Not wanting to exercise or play
- Having trouble going up or down steps
- Stumbling
- Acting lethargic

CONCLUSION

YOUR NEW LIFE WITH YOUR HUSKY

The most important thing you can do for your husky, with regard to any behavioral issues, is to establish the ground laws from the outset.

Setting yourself up as the leader isn't about arrogance or bossiness; it's about creating an environment that your dog expects and feels comfortable with. Allowing your dog to rule the roost is not in his interest – it creates a dangerous situation that puts you, your family and others at risk. You wouldn't allow your child to dictate your household rules, so why would you allow your dog to do so?

If you've follow the guidance laid out for you in this A to Z guide, then there is a good chance you'll be able to correct your husky's behavioral issues alone.

However, if you are unable to improve your husky's behavior substantially, then seek assistance from a behavioral specialist or obedience school. There is nothing wrong with asking for help if will result in your lovable pooch being a positive asset to your household.

All in all, remember to enjoy life with your husky. Their time is short – why not make it the best it can be?

THANK YOU FOR READING

Thank you for reading this guide. I hope it helped answer any questions about owning a Husky puppy and set you in the right path of a happy relationship with your new family member.

Join our Facebook Group to share your experiences and tips with our fellow community members.

https://www.facebook.com/groups/huskypuppytraining/

27631713R00018

Printed in Great Britain
by Amazon